THE

SEVEN LAST THINGS

A Study Guide on Revelation 19–21

by
Gregory C. Benoit

ECS
MINISTRIES
The Word to the World

The Seven Last Things Study Guide
copyright 2004 by ECS Ministries

Published by ECS Press
ECS Ministries, Dubuque, IA 52001
www.ecsministries.org

Cover and text design by Gregory C. Benoit Publishing
Old Mystic, CT 06372

www.gregwa.com

ISBN 1-59387-004-3

Contents

INTRODUCTION

This book is intended to be a study companion to *The Seven Last Things* by David J. MacLeod (Emmaus College Press, 2003). The purpose of this study guide is to help the student to go deeper into the Scriptures, seeking to understand what God has to say concerning the future: the Second Coming of Christ, the millennial kingdom, the reality of hell, the new heaven and new earth, and God's will for men in all ages.

Revelation chapters 19–21 are the Bible's key passages concerning the final events of human history, including the return of Christ and the final defeat of Satan. These chapters are often referred to as "the seven last things."

The book of Revelation is sometimes intimidating, because it is difficult to separate out the figurative from the literal. There are portions of the book which contain word pictures that are intended to give a sense of some deeper abstract truth. An example of this might be the references to Jesus as a Lamb or to Satan as a serpent. On the other hand, there are certainly things which are to be taken literally, such as the reality of Satan or the triumph of Jesus over death and hell.

In the course of this study we will attempt to discern these differences. We will discover, for example, that hell is a very literal and real place, not some metaphor for suffering. We will see that Jesus Himself will return bodily to set up a kingdom on earth for a thousand years, physically and literally living on earth with His saints. We will look at Babylon as both a literal city that once existed—and probably will again—and also as a figurative symbol of the pride of mankind.

One thing will definitely emerge from this study: the events prophesied by John are imminent. The United States' war in Iraq and its subsequent rebuilding, for example, point to the real probability that Babylon is about to emerge as a world power once again. Throughout our examinations, we will always return to the question, "How should God's people be living in this world?"

Personal Devotional or Group Study Guide

This book can be used for personal Bible study as an aid in looking deeply into the seven last things of Revelation. The first group of questions in each study assist in *analyzing* what the Scriptures say and what they mean, while the second group of questions are intended to help in *applying* the principles of Scripture to our daily lives. In this way, we ask the Lord to show us "what does this mean," and "what does this mean to me."

However, this study will be much more valuable when it is used in a small group setting, where "iron sharpens iron" as fellow believers dig into God's Word together. In this setting, the student will be challenged to consider things that might have eluded him otherwise, and men and women can face some of the deeper questions together. More importantly, believers can pray together as they consider the truths of Revelation, supporting one another and holding one another accountable.

Each study contains far too many questions to be covered properly in a one-hour study. For this reason, each person in the group should go through each lesson ahead of time, together with the associated chapter of *The Seven Last Things*, coming to the study prepared for questions and discussion. The leader should select five or six questions from each category (analysis and application) to discuss, but should also be prepared to discuss those issues which others have found compelling.

A COMPANION

Regardless whether this study is used privately or in a group, the reader will get the most from it by reading *The Seven Last Things* as well. You will find references to it as SLT in the notes and in text. The notes section in each study is intended to help the reader in deeper analysis; numbers of the notes refer to the Scripture verses. All quotations are taken from the New American Standard Version.

The questions in this guide are intended to drive the reader deeper into God's Word, using it as a mirror to examine his own soul. Therefore, one will not always find direct answers to the questions in Dr. MacLeod's book, yet one will find insight and guidance which will prove invaluable in understanding the book of Revelation.

7

❧ NOTES ❧

The Fall of Babylon
Revelation 18

Our study opens with the fall of earth's greatest city, Babylon, known in Revelation as the "great prostitute." Babylon was once a great center for trade and international influence, and she will become so once again in the time leading up to the last days—an event that has possibly already begun in the early days of the 21ST century.

In the course of time, the city will become a symbol of all that is wicked in the systems of man, centered on man's inherent greed for power and possessions. Babylon also presents a figure for the pride of mankind, much as Babel was in the days following Noah.

In this chapter we will witness the terrible destruction of that great city, and we will see the dreadful effect that it has on the people of the world. We will also see the reaction of heaven to the destruction, and that response is quite different from the viewpoint of unregenerate man.

Read Revelation chapter 18 and consider some of the following questions. This chapter, while not directly covered in *The*

Seven Last Things (SLT), is included for extra background on the subsequent material.

⚜ ANALYSIS ⚜

1. What is Babylon's great crime? Why has she come under God's wrath?

2. What is the "wine of the passion of her immorality" (v. 3)? What does it mean to drink of that wine?

3. How would "all the nations have drunk" of it?

4. Why does God command His people to "come out" of Babylon (v. 4)? Does this mean that there will be believers living in Babylon in the last days? If not, what does it mean to "come out"? If so, are they wrong to live there?

5. What is the meaning of Babylon's boast in verse 7? What does the boast reveal of Babylon's attitude toward God?

6. Why are the people of the world—kings, merchants, sailors—dismayed by Babylon's destruction? What does this grief reveal about their priorities and loyalties?

7. Read through the list of merchandise that is bought and sold in Babylon. How would you describe the sort of trade that is conducted there?

8. How might a city buy and sell "human lives" ("bodies and souls of men" (NIV))?

9. What is "the wealth of her sensuality" (v. 3)? What is sensuality? How does it differ from legitimate enjoyment of pleasures?

❧ APPLICATION ❧

1. Does Babylon remind you of any cities or nations in the world today? If so, which ones and how do they resemble Babylon? If not, what makes Babylon different?

2. What sorts of "adulteries" are committed in the name of free trade today?

3. In what ways do Christians face the risk of joining in such adulteries? How can we "come out" from that aspect of modern culture?

4. How can we as Christians participate in daily life and commerce without drinking "the wine of the passion" of Babylon?

5. Where do you find your security in life? Do you feel secure against calamity? Do you view yourself as a helpless "widow" (v. 7)?

6. What exactly does it mean to glorify oneself (v. 7)? How might a Christian fall into this sin?

7. How does a Christian guard against sensuality? How do we draw a line between this and the basic pleasures of life?

8. Where do we draw the line between meeting the legitimate needs of life and living in excessive luxury? Where does your own life fall on this line?

9. Does contemporary America have any of Babylon's traits? Your church? Your own life?

7

✧ RESPONSE ✧

Spend some time in prayer, asking the Lord to show you areas in your own life which might reflect the values of Babylon. Ask Him to help you in making His values your own.

✧ NOTES ✧

2   **Babylon the great.** Babylon is used here both literally and figuratively. In a figurative sense, the city represents the pride of man, building and scheming and reaching for power. She is similar in this sense to Babel, where man thought that he could reach heaven by his own creations—an attitude which still prevails in modern society. Literally, however, it is very likely that the city of Babylon, located in modern Iraq, will be rebuilt to become an international center of commerce and influence. The United States' war with Iraq, and its subsequent rebuilding, are likely to be the beginning of this event.

3   **wine of the passion of her immorality.** Sexual immorality and hedonistic excesses will undoubtedly come to characterize the rebuilt Babylon, even as they did in the Babylon of Daniel's day (Dan. 4:28 ff). On a larger scale, man is notoriously unable to remain godly in times of great prosperity; success, possessions, and power are intoxicating and addictive. When Babylon becomes the center for world trade, she will lead all nations into her idolatries of materialism, greed, and debauchery.

4   **Come out of her, my people.** The Lord calls His chosen ones to leave Babylon. This may be literal, indicating that there will be believers living in Babylon prior to her great destruction, or it may be figurative, a timeless warning to Christians to be "in the world but not of it." Either way, God's people must "be self-controlled and alert" (1 Pet. 5:8) to avoid the idolatries of the world, regardless of when or where they live.

7   **she says in her heart.** Here again we see the terrible pride of man—a pride which is merely self-deceit, persuading himself that he can be his own god. To say that "I sit as a queen" is to boast to oneself that I am the master of

my own destiny, the same foolish boast which Lucifer once made, as we shall see in future studies. This is the exact sin of pride which our culture commits today in "learning to love ourselves" and putting our faith in military and medical technology.

11   the merchants of the earth weep and mourn. The world will indeed weep and mourn over the terrible destruction of Babylon, but their grief will be for their own loss, "because no one buys their cargoes anymore." There is a chilling lack of concern here for the men, women, and children who have been burned alive in the great cataclysm.

20   Rejoice over her, O heaven! At first, it would seem that heaven also has no concern for the lost souls of Babylon, going even further than the earthly merchants by rejoicing over the destruction. In reality, however, the heavenly hosts will rejoice to see God's holy justice triumph over the wickedness and injustice of the world. God's holiness includes perfect justice and righteousness, and it is cause for rejoicing among His people when He displays His glory and power over the forces of darkness.

✺⸿ FURTHER READING ⸿✺

Johnson, Alan F. "Revelation." In *The Expositor's Bible Commentary*, Frank E. Gaebelain, ed. Grand Rapids: Zondervan, 1981.

Notes

2

⟡

HEAVEN'S HALLELUJAH CHORUS
REVELATION 19:1–10

⟡

As chapter 19 opens, we move from the events on earth to the response in heaven. Babylon, a great city teeming with human life and endeavor, has been utterly destroyed, and only her smoking rubble remains.

The reactions in heaven, however, may surprise us. While the people of earth wail and lament and throw dust on their heads, the hosts of heaven are rejoicing. John recounts for us two great "hallelujah choruses," sung by saints and angels alike. The cause of these hymns is twofold: Babylon is destroyed, and the wedding feast of the Lamb is about to begin.

There is an interesting contrast here between the destruction of Babylon and the wedding feast for Christ and His bride, just as there is a strong difference between the bride and the great prostitute of chapter 18. We will compare these in detail in this study.

Read Revelation 19:1–10 and *SLT* introduction, then consider some of the following questions.

7

ANALYSIS

1. What does it mean that salvation belongs to God (v. 2)? Glory? Power?

2. How is God's destruction of Babylon both "true and just" (v. 2)?

3. Do you think that Babylon is symbolic or a literal city? If symbolic, explain the symbolism. If literal, explain why God's servants rejoice in her destruction.

4. Why does the "wedding of the Lamb" (v. 7) follow the destruction of Babylon? Why must Babylon be destroyed before the wedding feast takes place?

5. Who is the bride of Christ? What does it mean that she "has made herself ready" (v. 7)?

7

6. Why is "fine linen" used as a symbol of "righteous acts" (v. 8)? What does this metaphor tell us about the nature of such righteous acts (e.g., value, purity, etc.)?

7. Who are invited to the wedding supper? Who are excluded? Find Scripture passages to support your answers.

8. Why does the angel command John not to worship him? Why did John try to in the first place?

9. Compare the bride of the Lamb with the great prostitute of chapter 18. Consider also Ephesians 5:25–27. What do you see in this comparison?

10. Note that the bride "was given" the fine linen to wear. (Some translations say that she is "permitted" to wear it.) What does this tell us about our own righteous acts? About God's grace?

7

❧ APPLICATION ❧

1. Have *you* accepted the Lamb's invitation to be part of the wedding feast?

2. Why would the heavenly hosts actually rejoice to see the utter destruction of a great city of men? How can it be godly to rejoice over the destruction of others? How does the heavenly response compare with that of the people of earth?

3. When is it appropriate for Christians to rejoice over the downfall of others? When is it inappropriate? Support your answers with Scriptural examples.

4. Why is God's wrath just? Why is this justice an important part of His plan for the redemption of His people?

7

5. How should we be making ourselves ready for the wedding feast? How righteous are the acts in your own life lately?

6. Are you in general living your life more as the bride of Christ or as a follower of the great prostitute?

7. How is marriage symbolic of our relationship to Jesus? With this in mind, how is compromise with the world comparable to adultery?

8. Are there things or people in your life who compete with God for your full devotion?

✧ RESPONSE ✧

Spend time in prayer, asking the Lord to help you see the things or affections which compete for your full devotion to Him.

7

❧ NOTES ☙

1   **Hallelujah!** See *SLT*, P. 4–5. This term means literally, "praise the Lord."

   Salvation and glory and power. These essentially encompass all that mankind strives for, all that we need. Wealth, security, power, even life itself are the essence of life's focus. Yet these are the private property of God. He alone can dispense them as He sees fit. All striving is vain for life, liberty, and the pursuit of happiness, apart from God.

2   **HIS JUDGMENTS ARE TRUE AND RIGHTEOUS.** See *SLT*, P. 6–7. The judgment of God, poured out in wrath on Babylon, is absolutely holy and righteous. It is prideful and wrong for men to say "I could never serve a God who kills people," or to draw a distinction between "the God of the Old Testament" and "the God of the New Testament." God's wrath has always been kindled by man's wickedness, just as His mercy and grace have always provided salvation.

5   **Give praise to our God.** It is, therefore, fitting that God's people praise Him for His justice and truth, even as we do for His grace and mercy.

7   **the marriage of the Lamb.** See *SLT*, P. 10–17. Consider the many ways in which an excited bride prepares for her coming wedding day, all geared to make herself desirable to her husband. The church is commanded to do the same, ensuring that our lives are pure and clothed in garments of righteousness.

❧ FURTHER READING ☙

Wood, A. Skevington. *Prophecy in the Space Age*. Grand Rapids: Zondervan, 1963.

3

❦

The Second Coming of Christ
Revelation 19:11-16

❦

In our last study, we saw the preparations for the great wedding feast, whose groom is to be the Lamb of God. This week, however, we will see the Lord in a very different pose, this time as the great warrior, the world's true ruler who governs with a rod of iron.

These two pictures may seem contradictory—a loving groom and a terrifyingly powerful warrior—but we must understand all of Christ's attributes if we are to have a clear picture of the character of God.

In this section, John describes the Second Coming of Christ, and the picture is dramatically different from His first coming. Jesus was born as a helpless human baby, living in poverty and obscurity prior to beginning His ministry. When He comes again, however, He will ride in on a great white steed as a conquering warrior to destroy, once and for all, His enemies.

Read Revelation 19:11–16 and *SLT* chapter 1, then consider some of the following questions.

7

✺C Analysis Cೞ✺

1. Who is the rider on the white horse?

2. What does it mean that His "eyes are like blazing fire" (v. 12)? What does this reveal about His character?

3. Why is He wearing "many crowns"? What does this reveal about His authority?

4. Why does the rider have a name that only He knows? Why is it written on Him?

5. What would "a robe dipped in blood" (v. 13) look like? What would it signify?

6. Whose blood is the robe dipped in? His own? His enemies'? Satan's?

7. Why do the rider and His army ride white horses? What is the meaning of the "fine linen, white and clean" (v. 14)?

8. What is the "sharp sword" which the rider wields? Why is it coming from His mouth rather than His hand?

9. What does a scepter signify? Why is He carrying a rod of iron instead of a scepter of gold?

10. Why is "the fury of the wrath of God Almighty" (v. 16) pictured as a winepress?

❦ APPLICATION ❧

1. Why is Christ called "the Word of God" (v. 13)? What does this reveal about His character? His power?

2. Why does John use this double emphasis, "the fury of the wrath of God Almighy"? Why not just "the fury of God" or "the wrath of the Almighty"?

3. Why would an army go to battle wearing linen instead of armor? Why are they not dressed here in the "full armor of God" which Paul describes in Ephesians 6?

4. Why is the King clothed in bloody garments while His followers wear spotless white?

5. What weapons do the army have? What does this suggest about the coming war against the Beast?

7

6. How does Christ's Second Coming compare with His first coming, when He was born in Bethlehem?

7. Why did Jesus ride into Jerusalem on a donkey (Matt. 21:5)? Why will He return on a white horse? How do we reconcile these very different representations of the Person of Christ?

8. How do the "many crowns" of Christ's Second Coming compare with the crown He wore at Calvary? What does this show us of the character of Christ?

9. If Christ's Second Coming is imminent, are you living daily in a way that will please or displease Him?

10. Are your own spiritual "garments" pure white or stained at present? How can you "whiten" your daily life?

11. What aspects of Christ's character move you to worship?

❧ RESPONSE ❧

Spend some time in prayer offering Him your worship and adoration.

❧ NOTES ❧

11   **white horse.** See *SLT*, P. 40–42. John mixes literal facts with figurative descriptions in this section. It is a literal fact that Christ will return in glory to establish His kingdom, but the visual descriptions which John uses here are probably figurative.

Faithful and True. See *SLT*, P. 42–44. We shall see repeatedly as we progress through Revelation that God's holiness is composed, not just of His mercy and grace, but also of His righteousness and justice. The Lamb is a picture of His grace and humility, but here we see a picture of His power and lordship. Both are equally a part of God's nature, and both are equally holy and pure.

12   **eyes are a flame of fire.** See *SLT*, P. 45. The pictures of Christ in His Second Coming here are metaphorical, figurative descriptions that convey aspects of His Person. Eyes that blaze with fire speak of wrath, the returning warrior ready to do battle with His enemies. It may also suggest the Lord's ability, as the Supreme Ruler, to discern truth with no element of error or prejudice (Heb. 4:13).

many diadems. See *SLT*, P. 45–46. The crowns (diadems) suggest the Lord's absolute authority over all dominions. It may also indicate that He has already won countless victories.

a name ... which no one knows. See *SLT*, P. 46–47 for a thorough explanation.

13 **robe dipped in blood.** See *SLT*, P. 48–49. Jesus won the final victory over death by shedding His own blood, so it would be fitting that He be robed in blood at His Second Coming. Yet He will return to destroy the forces of Satan and, as we shall see in future passages, this includes the shedding of His enemies' blood. The blood-dipped robe speaks of a powerful warrior who has been victorious in terrible conflicts.

Word of God. See *SLT*, P. 49–50. Jesus is "the Word made flesh." This is a common theme for John, whose gospel begins by paraphrasing Genesis 1: "In the beginning was the Word, and the Word was with God, and the Word was God." God merely spoke at creation, and His Word became reality. In His Second Coming, Christ will merely speak and His foes will be undone.

14 **fine linen.** See *SLT*, P. 50–51. It is significant that the warrior's army are completely unarmed. They have no further need of armor, however, because the fight is finished, the war is over. Only Christ Himself will do battle here, and it will be short and decisive. The army is in fine linen because they are rejoicing, on their way to the wedding feast (19:7–9); it is pure and white because they have all been washed spotless in the blood of the Lamb.

15 **sharp sword.** See *SLT*, P. 52–53. Compare Hebrews 4:12, where God's Word is described as a sword. This is emphasized here by the fact that the Warrior's sword is in His mouth instead of His hand. The hand would suggest the concept of work, but Christ finished His work on the cross. His Word, however, lives forever, and it is omnipotent.

rod of iron. See *SLT*, P. 53. The scepter (translated here as "rod") is a symbol of a king's authority, representing both his justice and his own power to enforce it. (It is derived from the mace, an ancient military weapon.) The iron suggests absolute inflexibility as well as the fact that it can be wielded as a strong weapon. A golden scepter is just for show; this one is very real and very functional.

wine press. See *SLT*, P. 54–55. Wine is produced, of course, by crushing grapes, and this has traditionally been done by walking on them in a large vat. This image is one of great and violent wrath, as the blood of God's enemies will flow out like juice from crushed grapes. Jesus will not return to earth as a meek and powerless baby, but as a fierce and terrible warrior, carrying out the holy wrath and justice of God.

16 KING OF KINGS, AND LORD OF LORDS. See *SLT*, P. 55–57.

FURTHER READING

Travis, Stephen. *I Believe in the Second Coming of Jesus*. Grand Rapids: Eerdmans, 1982.

MacDonald, George. *The Gifts of the Child Christ*. Grand Rapids: Eerdmans, 1973.

THE DEFEAT OF ANTICHRIST
REVELATION 19:17-21

The great prostitute of Babylon has been destroyed, amidst great rejoicing in heaven. But what about the Beast and his wicked hosts? The people of Babylon were not alone in defying the Almighty God.

John tells us that, immediately after the fall of Babylon, God turns His wrath toward the rest of mankind, the followers of the Antichrist. Once again we have a vivid and grisly picture of the destruction that is to come, with a second great feast. This feast, however, is quite unlike the wedding feast of our previous study. This time, the invited guests are vultures, and the menu is the flesh of dead men.

Read Revelation 19:17–21 and *SLT* chapter 2, then consider some of the following questions.

7

❧ ANALYSIS ❧

1. Why is the angel pictured as "standing in the sun"? Why not on the moon or atop a high mountain?

2. To what sort of feast is the angel inviting the birds of the air? How does this feast compare with the "wedding supper of the Lamb" (v. 9)?

3. In what sense is this feast a fitting "celebration" for the Beast and his followers? In what sense is the wedding supper of the Lamb fitting for Christ and *His* followers?

4. Why is this gruesome feast referred to as "the great supper of God" (v. 17)? Why not "the great supper of Satan"? How can such a thing bring glory to God?

THE SEVEN LAST THINGS 28

5. How does the "menu" of this terrible supper compare with that of the Lord's last supper (Matt. 26:26–28)? In what sense have the followers of the Beast shared in a sort of unholy communion with the evil one?

6. Who is "the rider on the horse" (v. 19)? Who is "his army"?

7. Why does the rider's sword come out of His mouth rather than swing from His right hand?

8. Verse 18 seems to indicate that virtually all people of the earth will gather to make war on Christ and His followers. How could such a thing take place? (Consider also Psalm 2:1–6, 2 Thessalonians 2:8–12, and Revelation 16:13–16.)

9. Enoch (Gen. 5:24) and Elijah (2 Kings 2:11) were both taken up to heaven alive. How do the Beast and his false prophet compare here?

10. How much of this passage do you think will be literally fulfilled? Figuratively?

❧ APPLICATION ❧

1. In what ways is the breaking of bread a symbol of the wedding feast to come (19:7–9)?

2. What human behaviors today might be symbols of the coming feast of the birds? How does Babylon exemplify these behaviors in chapter 18?

3. How are the Beast and his army destroyed? What sort of harm do they do to God's army in this attempt at war?

7

4. How can a loving, merciful God cast people into hell? How do we reconcile this with Ephesians 2:14–18?

5. What does this passage reveal to us of God's utter power over Satan and the world? How is it encouraging that He is able to defeat the enemy so easily, with the mere power of His Word?

6. The army of Satan apparently never even strikes a blow against God's army. How can God's people find comfort from this prophecy during times of persecution?

7. Which "supper" will you be attending: the supper of the Lamb, or the supper for the birds of the air? On what do you base your answer?

8. How much power does God's Word have in your life today?

9. The people of earth will be "deluded" by the Antichrist. Are there any worldly teachings or values which have deluded you from God's truth? How can you know what is true (1 John. 4:1–6)?

✣ Response ✣

Spend time in prayer, asking the Lord to reveal any areas in your own thinking which have been deluded by the lies of the world.

✣ Notes ✣

17 **standing in the sun.** See *SLT*, P. 77. This may be figurative or it may be literal. Figuratively, the sun represents a point above and apart from earth, giving the angel a view of the entire globe without being part of it. While the moon waxes and wanes, the perspective of God never changes or vacillates.

the great supper of God. See *SLT*, P. 78–80. This is the gruesome antithesis to the "wedding supper of the Lamb" of chapter 19. The book of Revelation gives us many such opposites as this, a reminder that the things of the world, and the work of the devil, are always an inversion of the truth of God. Note, also, that this is the great supper *of God*—not of Satan. This horrible judgment is a deliberate part of God's eternal plan, satisfying His holy justice. God will not ignore the wickedness of men.

18 **eat the flesh.** See *SLT*, P. 78–80. Here we have another such inversion. Jesus instituted the Lord's Supper (Matt. 26:26–28) as a symbol of what it means to become one with Himself, eating His flesh and drinking His blood.

As Christians, our communion with God is intensely intimate, as we seek to make His Word the central point in our lives. Those who follow the teachings of the world make the lies of Satan the basis of their lives, whether or not they realize it. In a figurative sense, those who reject Christ partake of an unholy communion with the world, which will become a literal reality in the last days. Dead bodies being eaten by vultures is an apt picture of the work of Satan and his followers.

flesh of all men. See *SLT*, P. 79. These are the unbelievers of all nations, those who have rejected the salvation of Jesus Christ. This entire passage emphasizes that the wrath of God and His judgment are integral to His holiness. John will continue to underscore this for us: that it is wrong to think that God's love and mercy have replaced His justice and righteous wrath, as though there were *two* Gods, one of the Old Testament and one of the New. The eternal damnation of those who reject Him is as much a part of His character as the free gift of salvation.

19 to make war. See *SLT*, P. 80–85. It seems utterly ludicrous to think that men would try to kill God with a gun, yet we did attempt it once with a wooden cross, so it is not so far-fetched to believe that our race will one day try again. Figuratively, this picture represents man's complete rebellion against God down through history, a rebellion which has always been as ridiculous as trying to shoot God. Yet this is more than a figurative picture here, and in the last days mankind will gather together his greatest army, armed with his greatest weapons to wage a literal military war on Christ—and will be defeated by a mere word.

20 he deceived. Satan is the great deceiver, the father of lies. One merely needs to listen to our media today to realize that he is still deceiving the world. As Christians, it is our duty to stand firm against the lies and deceptions of the world. John commands us elsewhere to "test every spirit" (1 John. 4:1), to constantly be alert to error and false teaching. This is not an option, yet it is too easy for believers to become complacent about truth, running the risk of themselves being deluded.

these two were thrown alive into the lake of fire. See *SLT*, P. 86–88. Here is another way that Satan has inverted God's work. Elijah and Enoch were "translated," carried alive into God's glory. The servants of Satan will receive a similar honor, being thrown—not carried—into the lake of fire.

21 the sword which came from the mouth. See *SLT*, p. 88–90. Man's greatest armies never fire a shot. Neither does God's army. Satan is destroyed merely by a word—by *the* Word. God created all things merely by speaking—He said, and it was. Similarly, He will destroy the works of the evil one forever by speaking, and they shall be no more. It is also significant that God's army is assembled, but only as spectators. We shall be there to witness His final victory, but we shall have no part in it. Satan shall be destroyed by Christ alone.

❧ FURTHER READING ❧

Graham, Billy. *Approaching Hoofbeats: The Four Horsemen of the Apocalypse.* Waco: Word, 1983.

Dyer, Charles H. *World News and Bible Prophecy.* Wheaton: Tyndale House, 1993.

THE BINDING OF SATAN
REVELATION 20:1-3

Immediately after the Beast and his armies are slaughtered, we watch with great joy as Satan himself is bound and cast into the great Abyss. In this section we will consider briefly just who Satan is, this great enemy of God and mankind.

The evil one began as a glorious being, one of God's higher orders of creation. However, he apparently forgot that he was just that—a creature of God—and thought he was capable of making himself greater than God. For this, he was cast out of heaven in humiliation and disgrace.

In the end, the evil one will be an object of scorn and derision for all of God's creation. John describes for us the beginning of his final destruction.

Read Revelation 20:1–3 and *SLT* chapter 3, then consider some of the following questions. We will also consider some other passages of Scripture to give us further background.

7

✦ ANALYSIS ✦

1. Why does God send an angel, rather than Christ, to seize Satan? What does this say about Satan's power and rank?

2. The word "devil" means divider or accuser. Why is Satan given this name? See also Job 1.

3. Why must Satan be released after a thousand years?

4. Read Isaiah 14:12–17. What was the sin which Satan originally committed? What was the result?

5. Satan aspired to be equal with God. In the end, how will he be viewed by all of creation?

7

6. Read Revelation 12:7–12. Why did Satan (the dragon) lose his war in heaven? What does this tell us about his power?

7. Why was Satan "thrown down" (12:9)? Why did God not simply throw him in hell right from the start?

8. How is Satan finally overcome?

9. Why is Satan's defeat brought about "by the blood of the Lamb and by the word of [the saints'] testimony" (12:11)? What does a Christian's testimony have to do with defeating Satan?

10. Read Matthew 25:31–46. What parts of Jesus' description are figurative? What parts are literal?

11. Does this passage teach that we become righteous by our works? If not, what *is* the Lord teaching here?

APPLICATION

1. When Satan is bound, what will be the effect on the people of earth? Judging from current events in the world today, do you believe that Satan has already been bound or that he has yet to be?

2. What is a dragon like? What are the attributes of a serpent? Why are these figures used to describe Satan?

3. Is your own personal testimony contributing to Satan's destruction? In what ways could your life become a more effective weapon in this spiritual warfare?

7

4. Read Luke 10:17–20. What does it mean that we have been given "authority to trample on snakes and scorpions"? How does a believer "overcome all the power of the enemy"?

5. Where do we find this power? Why are we not to rejoice in that power, but in the fact that our names "are written in heaven"?

6. Read 1 Peter 5:8–9. Why is Satan depicted here as a lion? What does this teach us about his character?

7. Why are we told to be *self*-controlled when fighting an enemy? Why alert?

39   STUDY GUIDE

7

✦ RESPONSE ✦

Spend time in prayer, asking the Lord to help you understand areas in your own life where you need to be more self-controlled and alert.

✦ NOTES ✦

REVELATION 20

1   **a great chain.** See *SLT*, P. 100–107. This chain is, perhaps, figurative rather than literal, since it seems unlikely that Satan could literally be bound with a mere chain. Either way, the event is literal in that Satan will be imprisoned in the Abyss for a period of time, preventing him from deceiving mankind.

2   **dragon ... serpent ... devil ... Satan.** See *SLT*, P. 108–109. A dragon is noted for its ferocity and greed, hating all living things except itself. Serpents have been perceived down through the ages as treacherous and sneaky, striking unexpectedly with their deadly poisons. The word "devil" comes from the Greek *diabolos*, which means "one who divides." All the names used for the evil one are figurative (he is not literally a dragon or a snake) to depict his evil nature. He is, however, a very real and very literal creature, as we shall see in the subsequent passages.

3   **abyss.** See *SLT*, P. 102–105 for the differences among hell, hades, and the Abyss.

ISAIAH 14

12   **star of the morning, son of the dawn.** Here we find yet more names for the evil one, but these refer to his original state before he rebelled. It seems that he was once a great and glorious creation of God, which makes his final state all the more pathetic and ridiculous.

13–14   I will ascend ... I will raise ... I will make myself. Satan's sin was pride, thinking himself capable of being equal with God. His ludicrous presumption here is equivalent to modern evolutionary theories ("I will make myself") and the contemporary culture of self-love ("I will raise my throne"). Yet Satan is merely a created being, like man and animals and fish, and is incapable of making himself something greater.

16   Those who see you will gaze at you. This is the ironic and just result of Satan's pride—to be mocked and derided by the rest of creation.

REVELATION 12

7   war in heaven. Verses 7 through 9 are commonly seen as taking place during the great tribulation period.

8   They were not strong enough. Satan, the great deceiver, began by deceiving himself. He thought that he could overpower God, but discovered that he couldn't even defeat the other angels. This is the nature of pride, deceiving ourselves into thinking more highly of ourselves than we ought. Again, it shows that the modern ideas of self-love and self-esteem are a deception of the enemy.

10   accuser. See Job 1 for a vivid—and probably literal—picture of how Satan accuses God's people.

11   they overcame him. This does not mean that the saints have destroyed Satan—that was done by Christ alone—but rather that our obedience, or testimony, defeats him in individual battles. Even at this level, however, the victories of the saints are possible only because of the blood of the Lamb.

FURTHER READING

Lindsey, Hal. *Satan is Alive and Well on Planet Earth.* Grand Rapids: Zondervan, 1972.

Pentecost, J. Dwight. *Your Adversary the Devil.* Grand Rapids: Zondervan, 1969.

Sanders, Oswald. *Satan is No Myth.* Chicago: Moody, 1975.

Notes

THE MILLENNIAL KINGDOM OF CHRIST
REVELATION 20:4-6

With Satan locked securely in the Abyss, the earth now enters a period free of his evil influence. This is not a permanent situation, however; it will last a thousand years. It is the period known as the Millennium.

It is at this point that the saints of God will rise from the dead to rule with Him on earth. This is the first resurrection; the second will come later. During the Millennium period, Christ's redeemed saints will sit in judgment on the affairs of earth; they will also act as priests for their God. We shall be, in short, intercessors and judges over the nations of the earth.

Read Revelation 20:4–6 and *SLT* chapter 4, then consider some of the following questions.

7

🙢 ANALYSIS 🙠

1. Who are the people who will be seated on these thrones of judgment? Whom and what will they be judging?

2. Why does John explicitly say that the martyrs "came to life" (v. 4)?

3. Who are "the rest of the dead" (v. 5)? Why do they "come to life" later?

4. This is the first resurrection. What will be the second? (See v. 11 and following.)

5. Why does John say that those of the first resurrection are "blessed" (v. 6)? What blessings do they enjoy?

6. What is the second death? Who will experience it?

7. What is the role of a priest? What will be the role of these saints if they are "priests of God" (v. 6) in the Millennium?

8. One job of a priest is that of "mediator" or intercessor. For whom will these priests act as mediators?

9. Why does John say that the saints "will be priests of God *and of Christ*" (v. 6, italics added)? Why does he state it this way?

7

✦❧ APPLICATION ❧✦

1. Do you know for certain that you will be raised in the "first resurrection"? On what do you base your confidence?

2. The saints of Christ will one day be called upon to judge the affairs of men. Is your own life at present a fit example for one who will sit in judgment?

3. What are you doing now to learn how to "rightly divide the word of truth"?

4. The saints of Christ will also serve as His priests. Is your life free from besetting sins? Are there areas of purity or holiness that the Lord would have you address in your own life?

5. How well are you interceding in prayer for others? Spend time now in prayer for unsaved friends and family.

7

❧ RESPONSE ☙

There are believers today who are facing persecution and martyrdom for their faith in Christ. Spend time now praying for them.

❧ NOTES ☙

See *SLT*, P. 135–137 for a complete overview of the major schools of thought concerning the Millennium.

4   thrones. See *SLT*, P. 137–143. The saints of God from all ages, from Adam through the future, will all be raised at the first resurrection (see below). They will serve as judges over the affairs of all nations on earth. See also *SLT* P. 184–185 for further discussion on the presence of the unsaved during the Millennium.

a thousand years. This is the period known as the Millennium. During this time, Satan will be bound in the Abyss, unable to deceive the nations as he has done since the Garden of Eden. However, there will still be sin in the world, as all men born during the Millennium will still be sons and daughters of Adam, bearing the sinful nature. Man in his fallen state does not need the evil one to find ways of sinning against God.

5   The rest of the dead. See *SLT*, P. 154–155. These are the men and women who have died in their sins, having rejected the salvation of Jesus Christ. We will witness this second resurrection in a later passage. The first resurrection is that of the saints of all ages, those whose sins have been covered by the blood of Christ.

6   priests of God and of Christ. See *SLT*, P. 156–157.

7

ᑐᑐᕁ FURTHER READING ᔋᕁ

Plantinga, Cornelius. *Not the Way It's Supposed to Be: A Breviary of Sin.* Grand Rapids: Eerdmans, 1995.

Erickson, Millard J. *Contemporary Options in Eschatology: A Study of the Millennium.* Grand Rapids: Baker, 1977.

7

⟨⟩⟨⟩

THE RELEASE OF SATAN AND MAN'S FINAL REBELLION
REVELATION 20:7-10

⟨⟩⟨⟩

The nations of the earth have lived in a nearly perfect world, a world governed directly by Jesus Himself who is physically present and visible on earth. The devil has been imprisoned, unable to deceive and tempt mankind any longer. After a thousand years of this, there can be little question that mankind will be different, finally free of hatred and bigotry and war.

This passage in Revelation will remove that false belief once and for all. Mankind will gather together, deceived anew by Satan, and will once again make war on the people of God. This terrible failure of man is all the worse since such a war will have already been attempted with ridiculous failure (the more so since God's saints have already died and risen again). We shall see that mankind cannot change so long as the fallen nature of Adam remains.

God will reveal once and for all that unregenerate man is hopelessly wicked. Without Christ, there is no hope of his redemption.

Read Revelation 20:7–10 and *SLT* chapter 5, then consider some of the following questions.

7

✦ Analysis ✦

1. Why does God release Satan from his prison? Why does He wait a thousand years to do so?

2. Why does Satan immediately set about trying to "deceive the nations"? Why has he not changed after a thousand years of imprisonment? What does this reveal about Satan?

3. Why do the nations of the earth gather for yet another battle against God, considering their utter defeat once before (19:19 ff)? What does this reveal about mankind?

4. Who exactly *are* the people who make war this time?

5. Who will be the people living in the city of God against whom the nations make war?

7

6. How does the battle compare with the one in chapter 19? How is it different?

7. This time Satan is thrown into "the lake of burning sulfur" (v. 10). How is this different from the Abyss?

❧ APPLICATION ❧

1. The devil deceived the nations of earth, leading them into battle. What sorts of deception might he use?

2. Read Genesis 3. How might Satan re-use these same tactics in his final temptation? How does he still use them in our world today?

STUDY GUIDE

3. Who is responsible for this final battle? Satan? Mankind? God?

4. Who is responsible for your own personal sins? How much blame goes to Satan for his temptations? How much to you for your choices? How much to other people? How much to God?

5. God has blessed the peoples of the earth with 1,000 years of divine rule, free of Satan's influence. What, then, does this final battle demonstrate about mankind?

6. Why would the God of grace and compassion throw Satan into a "lake of burning sulfur" where he "will be tormented day and night forever and ever"?

7

⁑ RESPONSE ⁑

Spend time in prayer, confessing areas of sin in your own life and asking for the Holy Spirit's help in overcoming those weaknesses.

⁑ NOTES ⁑

7   Satan will be released. See *SLT*, p. 183–192. Mankind has enjoyed a full thousand years free from Satan's meddling and deceit. He has lived in the most perfect earthly environment since the Garden of Eden, and has been enlightened to the truth of God's grace and love under the teachings of none other than His own Son. If mankind had any potential for goodness and righteousness whatsoever, it would certainly come to light now.

8   will come out to deceive. See *SLT*, p. 192–195. Satan charges out of the Abyss like an angry lion from a cage, instantly resuming the only work he has ever performed: lying. This is all that Satan is capable of, and he sets about it with vigor to make up for lost time. Satan will never change, and he will never be redeemed.

gather them together for the war. In this final moment, mankind proves once and for all that we are all, apart from the deliberate work of God, incapable of any righteousness whatsoever. Frank Sinatra may have done it "his way," but there will be no one singing that tune before the throne of God. Man's final attempt at rebellion is especially pathetic. After the amazing failure of the previous war on God (19:19 ff), how could anyone try again? To make it worse, how does one kill those who have already died?

Gog and Magog. See *SLT*, p. 194–195.

7

❧ FURTHER READING ☙

Davies, D.R. *Down Peacock's Feathers: Studies in the Contemporary Significance of the General Confession.* NY: Macmillan, 1944.

The Last Judgment and the End of the World
Revelation 20:11-15

This section is, in one sense, the most tragic and saddening in our study. In it we will witness the damnation of the uncountable souls who have rejected the grace of God. This takes place before the Great White Throne, the judgment seat of Christ where the book of life will be opened. All whose names are not written in that blessed book shall be thrown into the lake of fire for all eternity.

This passage is sad in the sense of the terrible tragedy of those who have rejected Christ. Nevertheless, it is also a glorious passage, in the sense that God's perfect justice and mercy have now been completely satisfied. Those who are cast into hell have *chosen* to go there; as C.S. Lewis writes, "the doors of hell are locked on the inside." God is finally allowing men to have what they have chosen, and His actions are just and holy.

Read Revelation 20:11–15 and *slt* chapter 6, then consider some of the following questions.

7

❧ ANALYSIS ☙

1. Who is seated on the Great White Throne? Why is the throne "great" and "white," rather than ornate and golden?

2. What does it mean that "earth and heaven fled away" (v. 11)? Why was there "no place found for them"?

3. Who are the people who stand before this throne?

4. What are these books which "were opened" (v. 12)? What is the "book of life"?

5. How can "death and Hades" give up their dead (v. 13)? How can death and Hades be "thrown into the lake of fire" (v. 14)?

6. What does it mean to die the "second death" (v. 14)? Could the saints reigning with Christ in the Millennium be killed in warfare?

❧ APPLICATION ☙

1. What does it mean that the dead were judged "according to their deeds" (v. 12)? These books do not determine who goes to hell, so what *do* they determine?

2. What is the lake of fire? Who is thrown into it?

3. Can a person be sure in this life that he will not be thrown into the lake of fire? If so, how? Support your answer with Scripture.

4. Is hell a real place, or is this picture of the lake of fire metaphorical? Support your answer with Scripture.

5. Will all souls one day be reconciled with God, or is hell forever? Support your answer with Scripture.

6. Why does God throw people into the lake of fire? How do we reconcile such judgment with the mercy and grace of God?

✺ RESPONSE ✺

Spend time in prayer, interceding for those you know who have not accepted God's plan of salvation through Jesus Christ.

✺ NOTES ✺

11 **great white throne.** See *SLT*, p. 218–219.

earth and heaven. See *SLT*, p. 219–221. In 6:14, John describes the sky "rolling up like a scroll." This could be figurative, suggesting that our earthly creation bows before His holiness, or it might well be literal, indicating the final destruction of our earthly cosmos and the beginning of a new heaven and a new earth. The literal approach gains credibility with the opening verses of chapter 21.

12 the dead. See *SLT*, P. 221–223.

books. See *SLT*, P. 223–227. These first books contain a record of every deed of every human standing before the throne. By these books the dead will be "judged according to what they had done." This is not the judgment concerning whether they go to heaven or hell; that will be done according to the book of life. This does suggest, however, that there will be varying degrees of suffering in hell. The deeds of men cannot bring them righteousness, but they do bring appropriate reward or punishment.

13 death and Hades. See *SLT*, P. 227–232. Here is great cause for rejoicing and worship, as God finally and irreversibly destroys the power of death over mankind. Death came in when Adam stood in sin, and it will go out forever when the last Adam sits in judgment.

15 book of life. This book contains, as it were, a record of righteousness, while the other books contained a record of works. Men write their own record of works by their actions in life, but only the Lamb of God will write the record of righteousness through His actions at Calvary. One's name will only be written in this book by God's hand and only if one has been redeemed by Jesus' blood.

lake of fire. See *SLT*, P. 230–231 for an excellent explanation on the existence of hell. Hell is a literal place of literal torment in which real people will suffer for all eternity. The language may be figurative, but the place described is very literal.

7

✦ FURTHER READING ✦

Lewis, C.S. *The Problem of Pain*. NY: Macmillan, 1944.

Kentzer, Kenneth and Carl F.H. Henry, eds. *Evangelical Affirmations*. Grand Rapids: Zondervan, 1990.

The New Heaven and the New Earth
REVELATION 21:1-8

Here at last we find ourselves in heaven. Death and Satan, enemies of mankind, have been permanently destroyed, and the eternal heavens have been opened. A startling picture is given of a completely new creation, wherein absolutely all things have been made new—a picture which puzzles our earth-bound minds. Yet this fades into unimportance when we discover the greatest gift of all: God Himself will be physically present and available to all His people for all eternity.

Gone forever is the age of "seeing by faith"; we will spend eternity being able to speak with God face to face, as one friend speaks with another. When one considers what this will be like, absolutely nothing else matters anymore.

Read Revelation 21:1–8 and *SLT* chapter 7, then consider some of the following questions.

7

✦✦ ANALYSIS ✦✦

1. What is the "new heaven" and the "new earth" (v. 1)? Is this literally a whole new creation, or is this a figurative expression for a new order of some kind?

2. Why is there no sea?

3. How can a city be "made ready as a bride adorned for her husband" (v. 2)? What does this picture suggest about the "new Jerusalem"?

4. What does it mean that God is "making all things new" (v. 5)?

5. Why does God say, "It is done" (v. 6)? How does this relate to Jesus' words on the cross, "It is finished"? What exactly is "done"? What exactly is "finished"?

6. Who is "he who overcomes" (v. 7)? What must he overcome to "inherit these things"?

7. Read through the list of people who will inherit "the lake that burns with fire and brimstone" (v. 8). What does it mean to be cowardly? Unbelieving? Vile?

8. What are "sorcerers"? Give examples of how sorcery and "the magic arts" (NIV) are practiced today.

❧ APPLICATION ❧

1. Who is the "bride of Christ"? Why is the new Jerusalem dressed as a bride?

2. What will it be like to have God Himself literally and physically living with us?

3. What might life be like if all of creation has a whole new physical universe with new laws of physics?

4. Why are "all liars" grouped together with "sorcerers" ("those who practice magic arts" [NIV])? Does this mean that everyone who has ever told a lie will go to hell?

5. Throughout these studies, we have witnessed the destruction of death and the opening of heaven. What part has mankind played in this whole process?

6. How do you picture life in heaven? Is your picture consistent with John's description here?

7. Will you be a citizen of the new Jerusalem? Explain your reasons.

≈ RESPONSE ≈

Spend time in worship, praising God for who He is—for His holiness, grace, and justice.

≈ NOTES ≈

1   **a new heaven and a new earth.** See *SLT*, p. 247–250. It seems that all of creation will be remade from scratch, the earth and heavens as we know them being completely undone. This may be a figurative description, suggesting a majesty and beauty beyond description, but the context strongly suggests a whole new creation, involving completely new laws of physics and matter. For example, in our present world nothing can move without some element of opposition and friction, but perhaps in God's new creation this law will be abolished and there will be no friction, no possible opposition.

no longer any sea. See *SLT*, p. 248–250. To paraphrase C.S. Lewis, if God takes away something from this creation, He will replace it with something much better.

2   **made ready as a bride.** See *SLT*, p. 250–251. The bride of Christ is His Church, not the city of Jerusalem. This may describe the city's beauty and splendor, or it may suggest that the bride herself—the saints from every age—dwells there.

3   **the tabernacle of God is among men.** See *SLT*, P. 253–255. This is the climax of all Scripture, the event that mankind has awaited and longed for since the Garden of Eden. Indeed, it will be a sort of return to paradise, as the entire physical universe will be newly created, and God will once again walk with man and speak with him face to face. (The NIV has "the dwelling of God is with men.")

6   **It is done.** Jesus cried from the cross, "It is finished!" At that moment the work of mankind's redemption was completed. However, the complete reality of our peace and fellowship with God will not be completed until He has made His dwelling with mankind, returning to "walk in the garden" with man again as He did before Adam's fall. God's promises of peace and joy are not mere metaphysical concepts; they are going one day to be literal, physical facts as His people join Him in the new Jerusalem. This part of God's plan is not yet done, and will not be done until the day comes that John is foretelling here.

7   **He who overcomes.** See *SLT*, P. 261–262. Jesus is the One who overcame Satan and death, and it is only through His "overcoming" that any man can enter the kingdom of God. Nevertheless, each individual must also overcome the evil one, as we saw in 12:11, by simple obedience and faithfulness to Christ. In this sense, those who overcome are all who have chosen to serve God instead of Satan, even as the martyrs chose faithfulness to Christ over life itself.

8   **cowardly.** See *SLT*, P. 262–266 for a complete treatment of this list.

⚜ FURTHER READING ⚜

Lewis, C.S. *The Last Battle*. NY: Macmillan, 1956.

Kreeft, Peter. *Everything Your Ever Wanted to Know About Heaven... But Never Dreamed of Asking*. San Francisco: Ignatius, 1990.

Notes

THE SEVEN LAST THINGS

68

Also available from
Emmaus College Press
(A division of ECS Ministries)
PO Box 1028
Dubuque, IA 52004-1028
(888) 338-7809
ecsorders@emmaus.edu

THE

SEVEN LAST THINGS

7

BY

DAVID J. MACLEOD

This is a first rate book which exhibits thorough research, helpful illustrations, and exemplary exposition of the biblical text—something desperately needed today.
Charles C. Ryrie, Editor, The Ryrie Study Bible, Professor Emeritus of Systematic Theology, Dallas Theological Seminary